BEAUTY SAVES THE WORLD

BEAUTY SAVES THE WORLD

A Contemplative Art Reveal
by: Tobias Taoh

Tobias Taoh

iUniverse®

BEAUTY SAVES THE WORLD
A CONTEMPLATIVE ART REVEAL   BY: TOBIAS TAOH

iUniverse books may be ordered through booksellers or by contacting:

iUniverse
1663 Liberty Drive
Bloomington, IN 47403
www.iuniverse.com
1-800-Authors (1-800-288-4677)

ISBN: 978-1-5320-6641-2 (sc)
ISBN: 978-1-5320-6644-3 (e)

Print information available on the last page.

iUniverse rev. date: 01/11/2019

Introduction

Humanity's most expansive intellect portrays exhibits delivers inspires more intricate theology science, Theo science, which incorporates capacity ability capability talent to express detail of spiritual the higher intellectual template within. The cogency to tap the within this template requires the holy way path of prayer, that one truth path of Jesus Christ, whom reveals to us in scriptural gospels as well ethereal esoteric spirit nuance the essence of eternal actuality as well the broader higher infinitude perpetuation.

We learn as we experience the body's own mind heart spirit resolve into the soul's provident intellect memory will resolution, together as quadratic toward octavation, numeracy in math of the cross, 4 quadrant, coagulating into 8 perpetuation, a 16 rhombo geometric, the essence of higher realms of seeing and hearing, both vision and sonar, grander sensibility, yet most cognizant an apparency character revelation.

We as human beings search decades of experience to make sense of our world through physical sense, when answered ability lies well within our soul's intellect to deliver the revelation so well sought as graciously received an enamor .

Dare we contemplate to let go of the world without to release reception of the cosmos within do our fingertips in a bowl of paint capture the expressed template so desired yet so touchable an evident predominant excursion to realms beyond heavens with god.

Untitled

Moses

Elijah

Passing

Bowl of Cherries

Education

George for Rushmore

Enlightened Bromeliad

Tropical

Crucifixion

Face

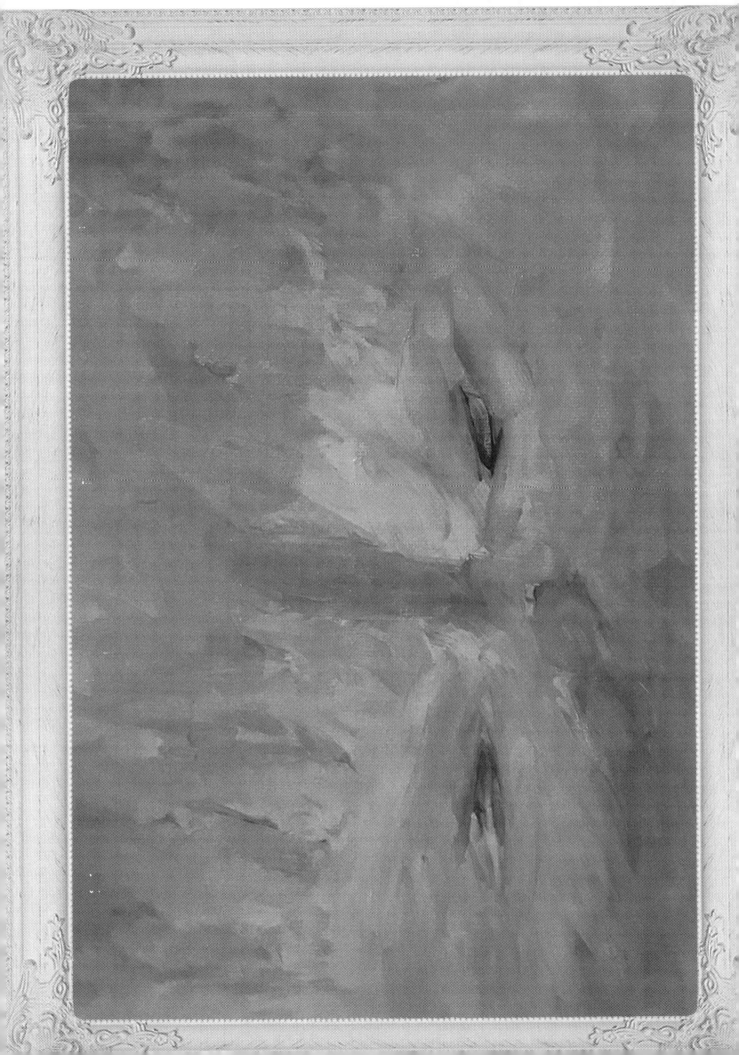

Eternal

Beauty no Death

Woman in Cave

Angels of Direction

Bed of Roses

Fire Below

Jeannie

Realm of God

Red Justice

Muted

Iota Little

Lamb

Saint of Cascade

Vault of Heaven

Infinitude

Golden

Masseucharist

Animal Kingdom

Yahweh

Printed in the United States
By Bookmasters